10-TASTIC FACTS!

IT TOOK **10** RESEARCHERS ABOUT **1,525 HOURS** TO FIND THE **3,500 FACTS** IN THE **WEIRD BUT TRUE SERIES.**

WOW!

NATIONAL
GEOGRAPHIC
KiDS

weird but true! 10

350 OUTRAGEOUS FACTS

NATIONAL GEOGRAPHIC

SCHOLASTIC INC.

The average rain

as much as

cloud weighs
100 elephants.

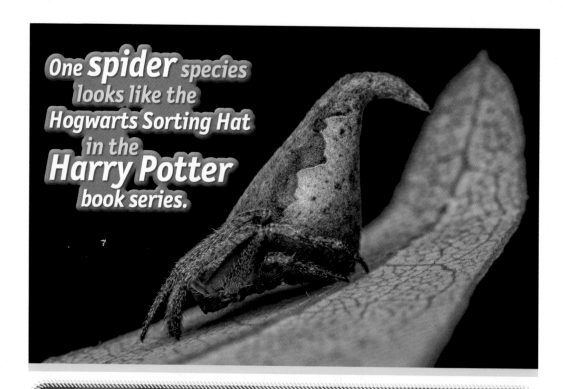

One **spider** species looks like the Hogwarts Sorting Hat in the ***Harry Potter*** book series.

ANCIENT OCTOPUSES HAD HARD SHELLS.

RESEARCHERS CAN TELL **WHAT SHAMPOO** YOU USE BY ANALYZING THE **CHEMICALS** ON YOUR **CELL PHONE.**

A U.S. company sells houses you can cover with **flower** and vegetable gardens.

Scientists made **artificial muscles** out of **onions.**

MOSQUITOES PEE ON YOU WHILE THEY SUCK YOUR BLOOD.

A cat named Bubba attends high school in California, U.S.A.

Feline
Bubba
12
A.S.B.
Leland
HIGH SCHOOL
2015   2016

Doctors removed a **14-** (6-kg) **pound hair ball** from a woman's **stomach.**

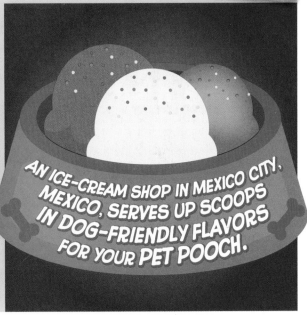

AN ICE-CREAM SHOP IN MEXICO CITY, MEXICO, SERVES UP SCOOPS IN DOG-FRIENDLY FLAVORS FOR YOUR PET POOCH.

A **HOUSE** IN NEW YORK, U.S.A., WAS **ENCASED** IN **ICE** DURING A **BLIZZARD.**

brrrrrrr

11

An **ancient drawing of a snake** in a Peruvian desert is longer than a **football field.**

A **BUMBLEBEE** TAUGHT OTHER **BEES** HOW TO MOVE A BEE-SIZE **BALL.**

?!

Scientists have begun to translate bats' language.

Some **bees** are purple.

meow

LIVE ON A HOUSEBOAT IN AMSTERDAM, NETHERLANDS.

St. Louis, Missouri, U.S.A., went from Spanish to French to U.S. rule in 24 hours.

AN ARCHITECT IN TEXAS, U.S.A.,

BUILT A HOUSE SHAPED LIKE A

COWBOY BOOT.

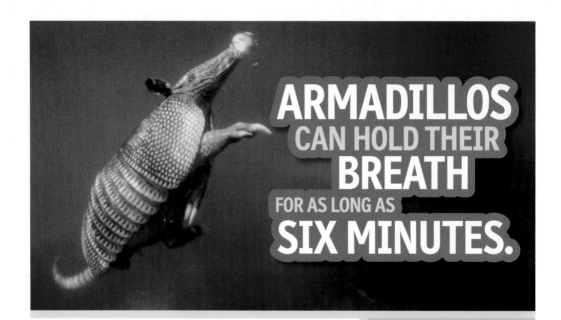

ARMADILLOS CAN HOLD THEIR BREATH FOR AS LONG AS SIX MINUTES.

SHREWS EAT ALMOST NONSTOP.

On average, there are **131 spiders** on every square meter of Earth. (10.8 sq ft)

There are more **book titles** on Earth than there are **different species** of living things.

SOME SCIENTISTS THINK NEW ZEALAND IS A MOUNTAIN PEAK ON A GIANT UNDERWATER CONTINENT.

A 16-YEAR-OLD BLACK BELT IN TAE KWON DO **SMASHED 111 CONCRETE BLOCKS** WITH HIS HEAD IN ABOUT 35 SECONDS.

A man repairing an **antique piano** found valuable **gold and silver coins** hidden inside.

A woman found her missing **wedding ring—** in her **dog's vomit!**

(IT'S BELIEVED THE RING WAS LODGED IN THE DOG'S STOMACH FOR AS LONG AS FIVE YEARS.)

oops!

People in Tibet put yak butter in their tea.

THERE IS A HIDE-AND-SEEK WORLD CHAMPIONSHIP.

In Tokyo you can have dinner at a **vampire-themed** restaurant decorated with **skulls** and **coffins.**

Fireflies are really **beetles.**

It can take as long as **two weeks** for a **wombat** to **digest** a meal.

An Italian artist makes life-size sculptures out of chewing gum.

ADDING **SALT** TO A PINEAPPLE MAKES IT **TASTE** SWEETER.

In 2015, workers *repairing a water leak* found a *time capsule* **Paul Revere** buried in **1795.**

SOME **BEES THROW UP** NECTAR TO KEEP THEIR **HEADS COOL** WHILE THEY **FLY.**

A **94-YEAR-OLD WOMAN** IN INDIANA, U.S.A., HAS BEEN WORKING AT THE SAME **MCDONALD'S** FOR MORE THAN **45 YEARS.**

FRENCH BULLDOG + PUG

FRUG

Lemons float; limes sink.

SCIENTISTS BUILT A $1,000 TREADMILL FOR SHRIMP.

Boaty McBoatface= an underwater research vessel named in an online poll

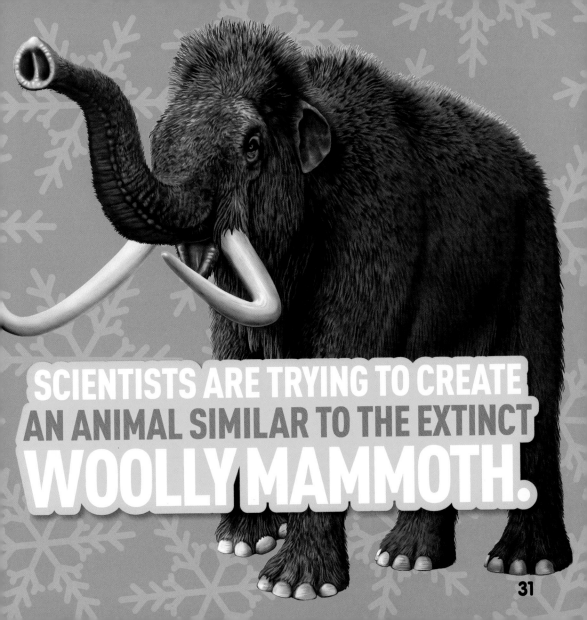

SCIENTISTS ARE TRYING TO CREATE AN ANIMAL SIMILAR TO THE EXTINCT WOOLLY MAMMOTH.

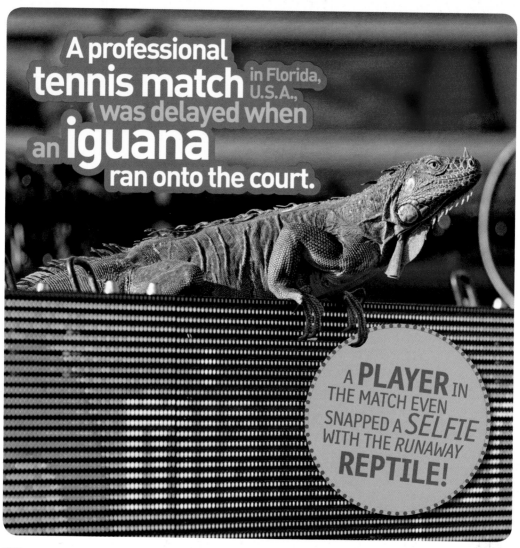

A professional **tennis match** in Florida, U.S.A., was delayed when an **iguana** ran onto the court.

A **PLAYER** IN THE MATCH EVEN SNAPPED A *SELFIE* WITH THE *RUNAWAY* **REPTILE!**

Taking a hot bath can be just as **healthy** as going on a **30-minute walk**, a study shows.

Butter has been around for at least **4,000** years.

MARGARINE WAS DYED PINK TO

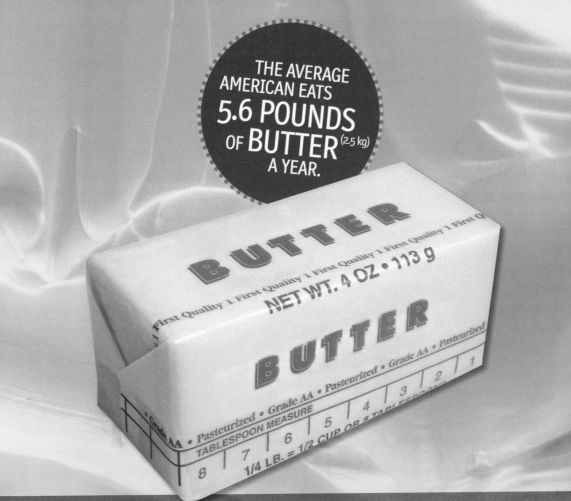

THE AVERAGE AMERICAN EATS 5.6 POUNDS OF BUTTER (2.5 kg) A YEAR.

DISTINGUISH IT FROM BUTTER.

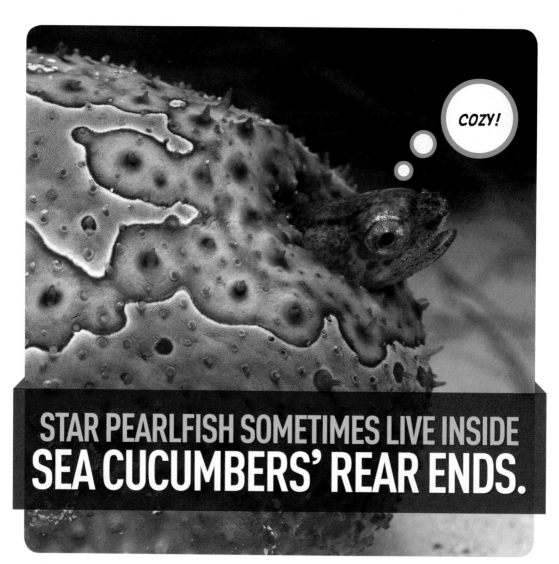

STAR PEARLFISH SOMETIMES LIVE INSIDE
SEA CUCUMBERS' REAR ENDS.

Three billion years ago, a **tsunami** as tall as a **skyscraper** may have swept across **Mars,** scientists believe.

A FIFTH GRADER ONCE TEXTED HER LOCAL POLICE DEPARTMENT'S NONEMERGENCY LINE FOR HELP WITH HER MATH HOMEWORK.

You can buy *perfume* that **smells** like kitten fur, popcorn, or earthworms.

37

THE WORLD'S FIRST SHIP TUNNEL—A MILE-LONG (1.6-km) PASSAGEWAY IN NORWAY'S STADHAVET SEA—WILL BE AS TALL AS A 15-STORY BUILDING.

THERE'S AN EMPTY CRYPT **BENEATH THE U.S. CAPITOL BUILDING IN WASHINGTON, D.C.**

SCIENTISTS **STUDY** FOSSILIZED **POOP** TO LEARN WHAT NEANDERTHALS **ATE.**

A group of **rats** is called a **mischief.**

SUDAN HAS MORE

AS PART OF A PROMOTION, A CHICKEN RESTAURANT **ONCE GAVE AWAY FREE FRIED CHICKEN BOUQUETS** ON **VALENTINE'S DAY.**

For about $70, you can send someone *a bouquet of roses made from* deep-fried bacon.

THERE ARE **10** TIMES AS MANY **GALAXIES** IN THE **UNIVERSE** AS **SCIENTISTS** PREVIOUSLY THOUGHT.

A British couple spent **10 YEARS** building a model **RAILWAY** throughout their **HOUSE** and garden.

THE **SKINNY HOUSE** IN LONG BEACH, CALIFORNIA, IS ONLY **10 FEET** (3 m) **WIDE.**

10 CONTESTANTS left in the wilderness for a reality TV show **STAYED FOR A YEAR** before learning that the show had been **CANCELED.**

AS OF 2016, ONLY **10 WOMEN** HAD EVER MADE **THE FBI'S MOST WANTED LIST.**

An **A10**-size piece of paper is **TOO SMALL** to write on.

A **CAR COMPANY** once made a **BOOK** that was **10 FEET** (3 m) **TALL.**

BETWEEN 1993 AND 2013, **10 NEW COUNTRIES** WERE CREATED.

$$1 + 2 + 3 + 4 = 10$$

The Korean alphabet has **10 VOWELS.**

10 POUNDS (4.5 kg) of **bat dung** was found in an **OFFICE CEILING** in Florida, U.S.A.

10 -TASTIC FACTS!

What? It wasn't just me!

45

The island of **Sumatra, Indonesia,** is the **only place where** **tigers, rhinos, elephants,** and **orangutans** live **together** in a natural habitat.

A bakery in Missouri, U.S.A., launched a doughnut 97,000 feet into space (29,565 m) using a helium weather balloon.

WITH A "PIE TOP" SNEAKER, YOU CAN ORDER PIZZA BY PRESSING A BUTTON ON THE SHOE'S TONGUE.

A COMPANY IN LOS ANGELES, CALIFORNIA, LIVE STREAMED A RACE BETWEEN A TORTOISE AND A HARE. (THE TORTOISE WON!)

1
2
3
4

Research found that **babies cry more** in Britain, Canada, and Italy than anywhere **else in the world.**

They **cry the least** in Denmark, Germany, and Japan.

At least 18 percent of pet owners **FaceTime** with their furry friends, a recent survey showed.

Baby humpback whales whisper to their mothers.

A SMALL MARBLE **COMPASS** ON THE CAPITOL BUILDING'S FLOOR

MARKS THE EXACT **CENTER** OF WASHINGTON, D.C.

The most common color of **penguin poop** is **pink.**

National **Animal** Crackers Day is on April 18 in the U.S.

A PACK OF
WILD
BOARS

WAS
SPOTTED
WANDERING
THE **CITY**
STREETS

IN SOPOT, POLAND.

About **4.5 million** years ago, **raindrops** made of **iron** fell on Earth.

You can get a **neck massage** by a **four-foot-long python** at a **hair salon** in Germany.

(1.2-m)

THE ISLAND OF MADAGASCAR SMELLS LIKE VANILLA ICE CREAM.

A frog uses its long eyes to help push food down its throat.

55

THE HAWAIIAN ISLANDS WERE ONCE CALLED THE SANDWICH ISLANDS.

THE AMOUNT OF **LICORICE MADE** IN THE U.S. **EACH YEAR**

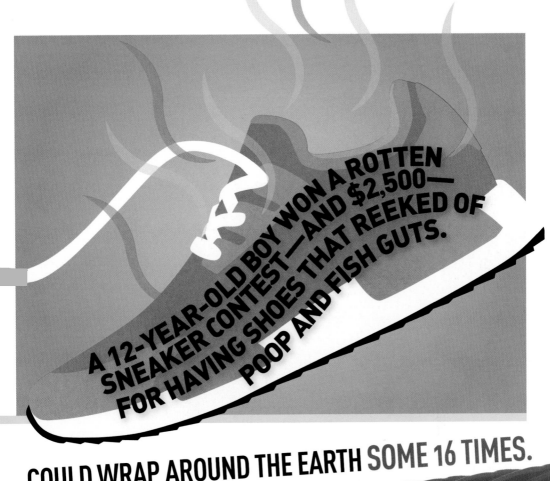

A 12-YEAR-OLD BOY WON A ROTTEN SNEAKER CONTEST—AND $2,500—FOR HAVING SHOES THAT REEKED OF POOP AND FISH GUTS.

COULD WRAP AROUND THE EARTH SOME 16 TIMES.

Rats and chimpanzees can laugh.

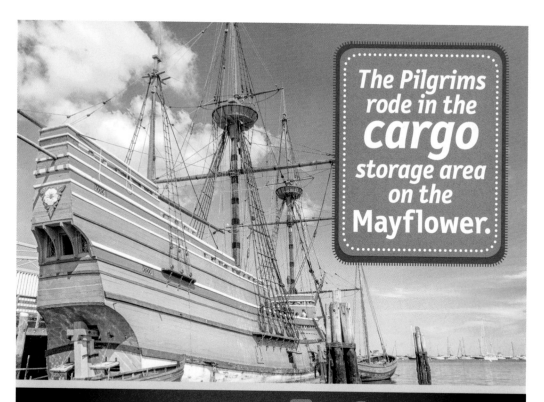

The Pilgrims rode in the **cargo** storage area on the **Mayflower.**

Researchers in **Egypt** found a **3,000-year-old fake toe** attached to a **skeleton's foot.**

THE U.S. MILITARY USED **SLUGS** TO DETECT **LETHAL GAS** DURING **WORLD WAR I.**

"*Beautiful*" and "*pneumonia*" are among the most **misspelled words** in the United States, according to a poll.

IN LESS THAN A DAY, A **SINGLE ROBOT** BUILT A **BUILDING** HALF THE SIZE OF THE **U.S. CAPITOL DOME.**

Engineers developed a bacteria-powered battery.

A TIGHTROPE WALKER COOKED AN OMELET OVER **NIAGARA FALLS** AND LOWERED THE DISH TO PEOPLE IN A BOAT BELOW.

During the **Vietnam War,** the U.S. used **fake dog poop** as secret **radio transmitters.**

There are giant **dust tornadoes** on **Mars.**

The **giant Pacific octopus** can have more than **50,000 babies** at one time.

NOW YOU TELL ME!

SOME LOBSTERS LIVE TO BE MORE THAN 130 YEARS OLD.

IT'S ILLEGAL FOR A DONKEY TO SLEEP IN A BATHTUB IN ARIZONA, U.S.A.

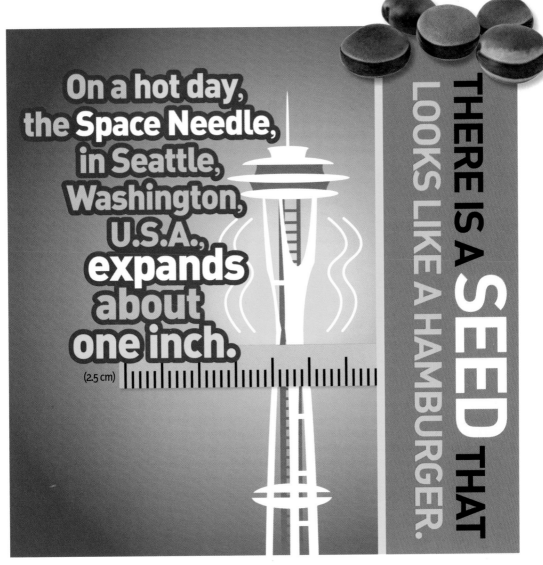

On a hot day, the **Space Needle**, in Seattle, Washington, U.S.A., **expands about one inch.**

(2.5 cm)

THERE IS A **SEED** THAT LOOKS LIKE A HAMBURGER.

BUMBLEBEES CAN RECOGNIZE EACH OTHER BY THEIR SMELLY FOOTPRINTS.

A restaurant in Paris, France, serves food flavored with dirt.

One item on the menu: a stew simmered with mud from the Seine River

THERE ARE **3,000 WORDS** IN THE **KLINGON LANGUAGE.**

YOU CAN LEARN KLINGON—
THE LANGUAGE SPOKEN ON *STAR TREK*—
AT A SCHOOL IN SWITZERLAND.

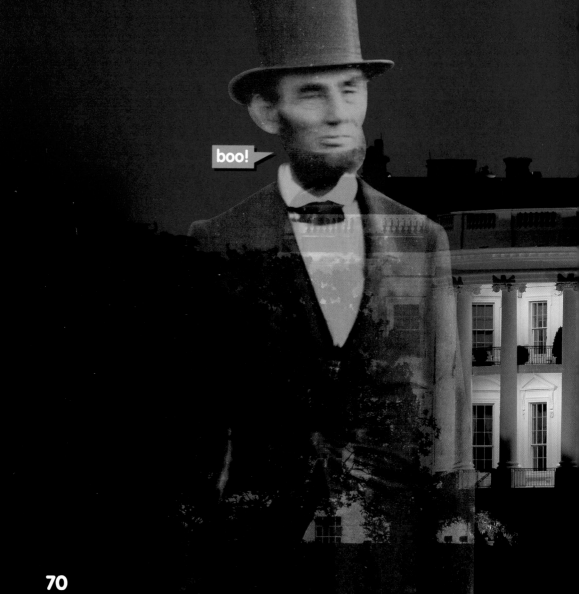

70

WHILE VISITING THE WHITE HOUSE, BRITISH PRIME MINISTER WINSTON CHURCHILL REPORTED SEEING PRESIDENT LINCOLN'S GHOST.

HENRY VIII OF ENGLAND BANNED MOST CITIZENS FROM PLAYING GAMES LIKE TENNIS, CARDS, AND DICE.

Chicken McNuggets come in just **four shapes:** the **ball**, the **boot**, the **bell**, and the **bow tie.**

SOME MUSHROOMS CAN MAKE THEIR OWN BREEZE.

Courting **seahorses** dance together every morning.

NINTENDO started as a playing-card company in 1889.

TERMITES ARE A SOURCE OF METHANE, A GREENHOUSE GAS.

SOME **CATS PURR** AS MANY AS **150 TIMES PER SECOND.**

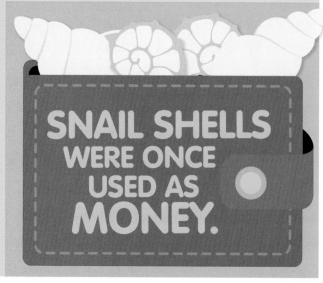

SNAIL SHELLS WERE ONCE USED AS **MONEY.**

A chess grand master played 326 games of chess at the same time. (She won 96.93 percent of the time.)

ABOUT **100 PEOPLE** COULD FIT INSIDE A BLUE WHALE'S MOUTH.

OPOSSUMS ARE ABOUT THE SIZE

OF A GRAIN OF RICE AT BIRTH.

They're so tiny that 14 babies can fit in a teaspoon.

WAX WORM
CATERPILLARS
EAT PLASTIC
SHOPPING BAGS.

A **woman** in Idaho, U.S.A., said **she wrecked** her **car** because she **saw Sasquatch** alongside the **highway.**

ONE **BRIDE-TO-BE** MADE HER **WEDDING DRESS** ENTIRELY OUT OF **FAST-FOOD WRAPPERS.**

Half of **Earth's** **water** is melted **space ice** that existed before **the sun.**

WOUNDS HEAL TWICE AS FAST **DURING THE DAYTIME** THAN AT **NIGHT,** ONE STUDY SHOWED.

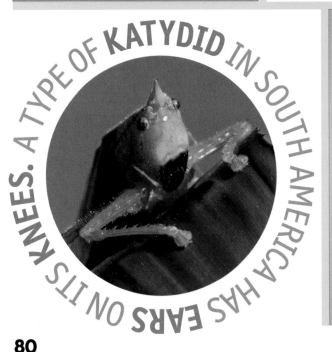

A TYPE OF **KATYDID** IN SOUTH AMERICA HAS **EARS** ON ITS **KNEES.**

Kindergartners in New Hampshire, U.S.A., *once hosted a* **wedding** *for their* **class ducks.**

A group of people in Massachusetts, U.S.A., **knits sweaters** for **chickens** to **wear** in the **winter.**

NASA'S SPACE POOP CHALLENGE OFFERED $30,000

FOR THE BEST WAY TO GET RID OF HUMAN WASTE IN SPACE.

BIG BIRD IS 8 FEET 2 INCHES (2.5 m) TALL—ABOUT THE SAME HEIGHT AS AN OSTRICH.

In **BOWLING**, three consecutive **STRIKES**—all 10 pins knocked down— is called a "**TURKEY**."

A **$10 BILL** has a shorter life span than a $1 BILL.

ALEXANDER HAMILTON, whose face is on the U.S. **$10 BILL**, was almost **BROKE** when he died.

A woman made a **DRESS** out of more than **10,000 STARBURST WRAPPERS**.

ONLY **10 PERCENT** OF AN ICEBERG IS VISIBLE ABOVE THE OCEAN'S SURFACE.

Queen Hedwig of Poland was only **10 YEARS OLD** when she was **CROWNED IN 1384.**

An **ARTIST** in Cleveland, Ohio, U.S.A., made a **10-POUND SCULPTURE** (4.5-kg) of basketball superstar **LEBRON JAMES**— out of **dryer lint.**

A Japanese **SPIDER CRAB** known as **BIG DADDY** measured more than **10 FEET** (3 m) **ACROSS.**

The **FIRST SPACECRAFT** to land on a **COMET** journeyed for **10 YEARS** before landing.

10 -TASTIC FACTS!

A **CRATER** IN SOUTH AFRICA WAS ONCE **10 TIMES** AS WIDE AS THE **GRAND CANYON.**

It takes **10 POUNDS** (4.5 kg) of **GRAIN** to produce **ONE POUND** (453 g) of **BEEF.**

That's Weird! ••

A **DOG** fell off his owner's **BOAT** into the ocean— then safely swam **10 MILES** to shore. (16 km)

ONE IN 10 of the **WORLD'S** known species live in the **AMAZON RAIN FOREST.**

THERE ARE MORE THAN 60,000 TREE SPECIES ON EARTH.

A library in Iowa, U.S.A., has **more than 4,000 tiny books,** many of which can be read only with a **magnifying glass.**

Someone once stole a **70-pound, $700** (32-kg) **popcorn ball** from a shop in Ohio, U.S.A. (It was later returned.)

IN 1936, A RUSSIAN SCIENTIST BUILT
A COMPUTER THAT RAN ON WATER.

The song "Mary Had a Little Lamb" is based on a true story.

OSCAR THE GROUCH USED TO BE ORANGE, NOT GREEN.

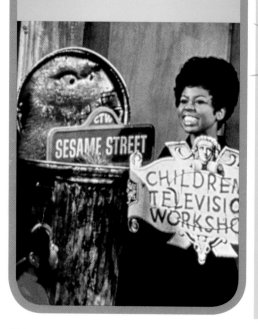

SESAME STREET

CHILDREN TELEVISIO WORKSHO

During World War II, British intelligence learned of a Nazi plot to kill **Prime Minister Winston Churchill** with exploding **chocolate bars.**

WOMEN ARE MORE SUSCEPTIBLE TO "CONTAGIOUS" YAWNING THAN MEN, A STUDY FOUND.

BLENNY FISH ESCAPE PREDATORS BY CRAWLING ONTO LAND.

The **seeds** of some **trees** cannot **sprout** unless they are exposed to **fire.**

A COLLEGE STUDENT IN JAPAN CAN **SNAP HIS FINGERS 296 TIMES** IN ONE MINUTE— A WORLD RECORD.

YOU CAN BUY A WEARABLE TENT THAT FOLDS UP INTO THE HEEL OF A HIGH-TOP SNEAKER.

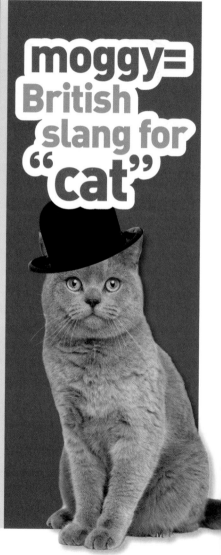

moggy= British slang for "cat"

A MAN IN BRISTOL, U.K.,
SNEAKS OUT AT NIGHT
AND CORRECTS THE GRAMMAR
ON SIGNS AND
STOREFRONTS

The amount of **chocolate** that **Belgium** produces each year weighs as much as **110,000 hippos.**

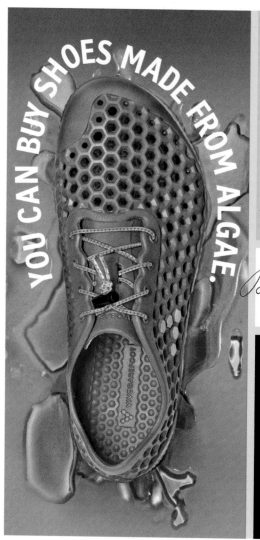

YOU CAN BUY SHOES MADE FROM ALGAE.

In 1738, a priest in France built a simple robotic duck that could eat—and poop out—a corn kernel.

Ben Franklin wrote a poem for a dead squirrel.

A PORTUGUESE MUSICIAN **CAN HIT A SINGLE PIANO** KEY A RECORD-SETTING **824 TIMES** IN **ONE MINUTE.**

In **World War II**, the U.S. used **inflatable tanks** and **rubber** airplanes to **fool** the Germans.

Police in California, U.S.A., found a man trapped in the chimney of the house he was trying to burglarize.

AN ALABAMA, U.S.A., COLLEGE STUDENT HAS MOWED 50 LAWNS IN 50 STATES— FOR FREE.

Some **ants** carry **umbrellas** made of **leaves.**

More than **half the world's tree species** are native to only **one country.**

Scientists made **bricks** from **Martian soil.**

One type of **gecko** has tear-away **skin** that helps it **escape predators.**

PREHISTORIC GUINEA PIGS WERE AS BIG AS COWS AND HAD A BITE AS STRONG AS A TIGER'S.

IN ANTARCTICA, HURRICANE-STRENGTH **WINDS** CREATE A RARE SCALY FORMATION CALLED **"DRAGON SKIN" ICE.**

The first English settlers to what is now North Carolina, U.S.A., **disappeared,** and no one knows what happened to them.

ORANGE PEKOE TEA CONTAINS NEITHER ORANGES NOR ORANGE FLAVOR.

IN 1958, CANADA **BLEW UP** AN **UNDERWATER MOUNTAIN** TO ALLOW SHIPS TO PASS THROUGH A CHANNEL.

A famous comedian donated more than **85,000 pages** of jokes to the U.S. Library of Congress.

IN TAIPEI, TAIWAN, **COMMUTERS CAN RIDE A CITY BUS** DECORATED WITH MOSS-COVERED SEATS AND LOCAL **PLANTS.**

THERE ARE RIVERS AND LAKES UNDER THE OCEAN.

A **shark** *photobombed* a 10-year-old Australian **surfer.**

CHIRPS=

CHIPS MADE WITH DRIED CRICKETS

THE **"GREEN FLASH"** IS A PHENOMENON IN WHICH THE SUN BRIEFLY CHANGES COLOR ON THE HORIZON AS IT RISES OR SETS.

THE BALL ON TOP OF A **FLAGPOLE** IS CALLED A **TRUCK.**

ONE STORE SELLS A PAIR OF JEANS COVERED IN FAKE MUD FOR $425.

TWO ARTiSTS in London, U.K., BUILT A **maze** MADE OF **250,000** *BOOKS.*

A BLACK **BEAR** BROKE INTO A HOME IN COLORADO, U.S.A.— AND **BANGED** ON THE FAMILY'S **PIANO!**

CATS CAN TURN THEIR EARS 180 DEGREES.

Martian meteorites have landed on Earth.

AN AFRICAN **ELEPHANT'S** DAILY AMOUNT OF **DUNG** CONTAINS MORE THAN 3,000 SEEDS.

You can buy a banana holder for your bicycle.

The town of Aladdin, Wyoming, U.S.A... population of 15, sold at auction for **$500,000**.

Nightingales can **sing** as loudly as a chain saw.

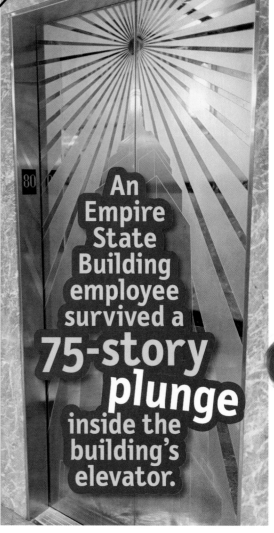

An Empire State Building employee survived a **75-story plunge** inside the building's elevator.

A NARWHAL USES ITS LONG TUSK TO STUN ITS PREY.

U.S. president *Thomas Jefferson* sometimes **wore a bathrobe** when meeting with *foreign diplomats.*

Air Force One contains a **mini-hospital** and an onboard **doctor.**

A **woman** in Florida, U.S.A., has a record-setting **collection** of **793 flamingo-**related items.

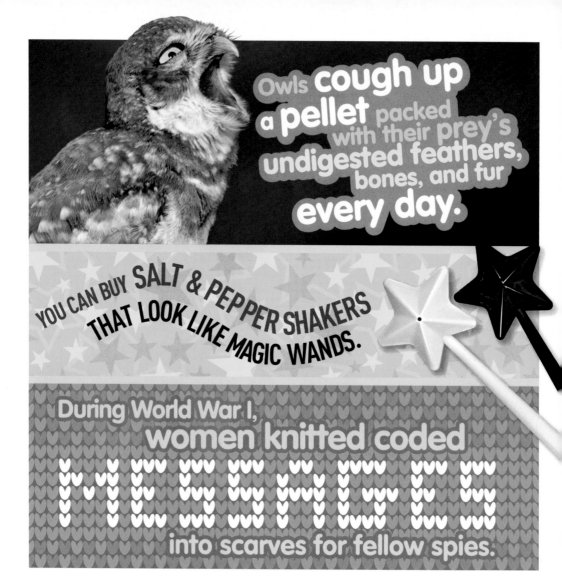

Owls **cough up** a **pellet** packed with their prey's undigested feathers, bones, and fur **every day.**

YOU CAN BUY SALT & PEPPER SHAKERS THAT LOOK LIKE MAGIC WANDS.

During World War I, **women knitted coded MESSAGES** into scarves for fellow spies.

FOUR
THOUSAND
YEARS AGO,
THE EGYPTIAN
PYRAMIDS
WERE SHINY
AND WHITE.

FIVE COUNTRIES IN THE WORLD ARE ON TWO DIFFERENT CONTINENTS.

EUROPE

Africa and Europe are only nine miles (14 km) apart at their closest point.

AFRICA

A **DAM** BEING BUILT IN TAJIKISTAN WILL BE TALLER THAN THE **EIFFEL TOWER.**

IT COSTS 19 CENTS TO PRODUCE A $50 BILL.

Ancient Romans sweetened their food with sugar made from lead.

Almost half the **gold** mined on **Earth** comes from one place in **South Africa.**

123

SCIENTISTS CREATED CYBORG PLANTS THAT CONDUCT ELECTRICITY.

A **10-FOOT-TALL,** (3-m) **bamboo-eating giant APE** prowled the Earth until about **300,000** years ago.

A Chinese construction **CREW** demolished **19 BUILDINGS** in just **10 SECONDS.**

There are **125 MILLION 10-YEAR-OLDS** around the **WORLD.**

It takes about **10 DAYS** TO MAKE **PICKLES** out of FERMENTED **CUCUMBERS.**

RED **M&M'S** WERE **BANNED** FOR 10 YEARS.

The number **10** WAS SACRED to **PYTHAGORAS,** A FAMOUS ANCIENT **GREEK** MATHEMATICIAN.

THERE ARE **10 HUMAN BODY PARTS** THAT HAVE JUST **THREE LETTERS:** eye, ear, leg, arm, jaw, rib, hip, gum, toe, and lip.

NINE out of **10 COUNTRIES** have at some point been invaded by Britain.

Paleontologists discovered a **PREHISTORIC**
SUPERCROC
that was as long as a
CITY BUS and may have
weighed as much as
10 TONS.
(9 t)

That's Weird!...

The original
ROMAN CALENDAR
had only **10 MONTHS.**

IT TOOK **10 MINUTES**
FOR A COMPETITIVE EATER
TO **gulp down**
62 HOT DOGS.

A **MAN** in South Carolina, U.S.A.,
claims to have been
STRUCK BY LIGHTNING
at least **10 TIMES.**

A BLINK OF AN EYE LASTS ABOUT
1/10 OF A SECOND.

A jaguar's **bite** is strong enough to dent a bowling ball.

Saying **"ow"** after you've been **hurt** may help you **tolerate pain,** according to a study.

A man was stung mid-flight by a scorpion that had stowed away in an overhead bin.

A pizza shop in Oregon, U.S.A., sold slices layered with more than 100 types of cheese.

IN THE NETHERLANDS...

YOU CAN SPEND THE NIGHT IN A DOCKSIDE CRANE—AND EVEN OPERATE THE CRANE.

A BUILDING IS DECORATED WITH CONCRETE EMOJIS.

YOU CAN BUY A **CUBE-SHAPED HOUSE.**

TOADS DON'T HAVE **WARTS**— **THOSE BUMPS** ARE **SKIN GLANDS.**

A **101-year-old man** became the **oldest** tandem **skydiver** by leaping out of a plane **15,000 feet** above the ground. (4,575 m)

(1.2-m)

THIRD GRADERS IN NEW JERSEY, U.S.A., DISCOVERED A FOUR-FOOT-LONG **BOA CONSTRICTOR HIDING IN THEIR CLASSROOM.**

The world's **oldest** bookstore— in Lisbon, Portugal— has been open since **1732.**

ANCIENT ROMANS MADE **PURPLE DYE** OUT OF BOILED **SEA SNAILS.**

One man spent **two months** making a **church** entirely out of **snow** in a remote village in Siberia.

In the 1800s, **COAL TAR** was added to **ketchup** to dye it **RED.**

A Los Angeles **ice-cream shop** uses a type of **charcoal** to create jet black **waffle cones** and soft serve.

A New York man once bowled **12 straight strikes** in 86 seconds.

A U.S. ASTRONAUT SET A RECORD BY SPENDING MORE THAN 535 CONSECUTIVE DAYS IN SPACE.

You can tell a **whale's age** by counting the **waxy layers** in its ears.

CAMBRIDGE UNIVERSITY IN THE U.K. HIRED A "PROFESSOR OF PLAY" TO STUDY LEGO PLAYING AMONG KIDS.

THERE'S A SECRET **BASKETBALL COURT** INSIDE THE MATTERHORN RIDE IN **DISNEYLAND.**

whee!

MOTHS LEARNED TO DRIVE A ROBOTIC CAR.

MORE THAN HALF OF THE **LONDON UNDERGROUND** TRAIN SYSTEM IS **ABOVEGROUND.**

Hyenas like to roll around and play in their own **vomit.**

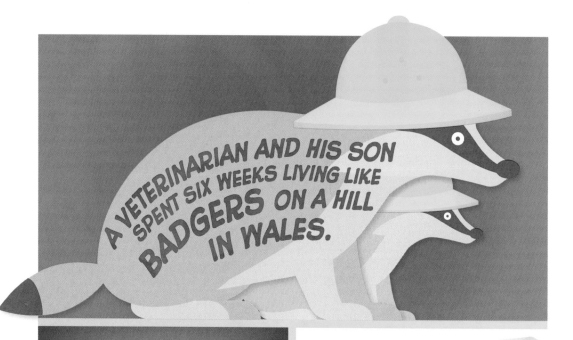

A VETERINARIAN AND HIS SON SPENT SIX WEEKS LIVING LIKE BADGERS ON A HILL IN WALES.

TINY BALLS OF FUNGUS AND MOLD CAN GROW IN YOUR SINUSES.

All mammals take about 12 seconds to poop, according to a recent study.

A **12-foot-tall** *(3.6-m)* **model** *of the* ***Washington Monument*** *is* **hidden** *in a manhole* *near the* **monument** *itself.*

A message in a bottle floated in the ocean for more than 108 years before washing up on a beach in Germany.

A rare white humpback whale was spotted swimming off the coast of Sydney, Australia.

A CEMETERY IN SLOVENIA SELLS **TOMBSTONES** WITH **DIGITAL SCREENS** TO SHOW VIDEOS AND SLIDE SHOWS OF THE DECEASED.

Janez Mlakar
1907 - 2000

THE **SCREENS** HAVE A MOTION SENSOR AND **TURN ON** WHEN SOMEONE IS NEARBY.

One company **dyes** its clothing with a mixture of silkworm **poop,** dried **beetles,** and **food waste.**

Pop star Taylor Swift accidentally released **eight seconds of static** on iTunes— and it became a **number one hit.**

IT TAKES FIVE YEARS FOR A SPACECRAFT TO TRAVEL FROM EARTH TO JUPITER.

EACH YEAR, THE WORLD'S **SPIDERS EAT** AN AMOUNT OF INSECTS **EQUAL TO TWICE** THE WEIGHT OF THE **HUMAN POPULATION.**

Astronauts grow vegetables in space.

LEECHES STORE THEIR VICTIM'S BLOOD FOR MONTHS AFTER A MEAL.

Some nudibranchs, a type of sea slug, can store algae in their bodies to collect energy from the sun.

A U.S. FAST-FOOD COMPANY IS TRYING TO SEND A CHICKEN SANDWICH INTO SPACE.

STONE AGE HUMANS HAD EARLY
VERSIONS OF DENTAL TOOLS
FOR TREATING CAVITIES.

One type of **bacteria** can repair **cracks** in **concrete.**

From 1928 to 2013, the letters **Q, W, and X** were banned in Turkey.

A secret message was discovered in Abraham Lincoln's pocket watch.

Pizza acrobats compete for **prizes** by tossing and spinning pizza dough.

More people snap **selfies in the city of Makati** in the Philippines than in any other place in the world, according to one study.

SCIENTISTS **BUILT NANOSCALE CARS** THAT CAN RACE ON A ROAD **THINNER** THAN A HUMAN HAIR.

A woman once **married the Eiffel Tower** after **falling in love** with the iconic Parisian landmark.

MORE THAN **20,000** **RATS** ARE WORSHIPPED AT A **TEMPLE** IN INDIA.

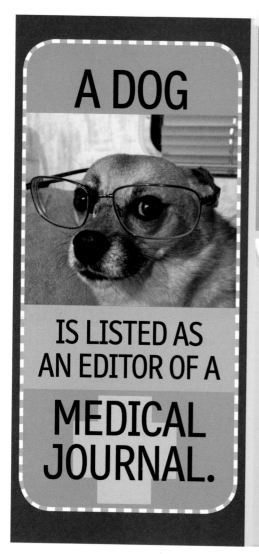

A DOG

IS LISTED AS AN EDITOR OF A MEDICAL JOURNAL.

IN 2015, EIGHT FEET OF SNOW FELL ON THE TOWN OF CAPRACOTTA, ITALY, IN ONE 18-HOUR SPAN.

(2.4 m)

SOME DRIED FOOD RATIONS FOR U.S. ARMY SOLDIERS CAN BE REHYDRATED WITH URINE.

William Shakespeare
"William Shakspere"
"Willm Shakspere"
"William Shakspeare"
spelled his name several different ways.

Scientists discovered a rare pink, scaleless fish that lives only in underwater caves.

AFRICAN ELEPHANTS SLEEP ONLY TWO HOURS A DAY, ON AVERAGE.

CORNSTALKS IN NEW YORK, U.S.A., GREW AS HIGH AS A FOUR-STORY BUILDING.

A woman in the U.K. claims she can predict the future by reading asparagus tips.

Legend has it that anyone who removes a *stone* from the island of Koh Hingham in Thailand will be **cursed.**

Ninety-four percent of dollar bills are covered with bacteria.

BlessU-2, a robot priest in Germany, can deliver blessings in 7 languages.

About **10 PERCENT** of land on Earth is covered with **GLACIAL ICE.**

FLEAS that infested **DINOSAURS** were **10 TIMES AS LARGE AS** today's fleas.

CRUSTACEANS with **10 LIMBS,** like crabs and lobsters, are also known as **DECAPODS.**

The **10TH PIN** IN **BOWLING** may have been added to get around laws that forbade **9-PIN** BOWLING.

THE WORLD RECORD FOR THE **WOMEN'S 100-METER DASH** IS 10.49 SECONDS.

The average **CHRISTMAS TREE** takes as long as **10 YEARS** to **GROW.**

An Austrian man set a world record by completing **29 BACKWARD SOMERSAULTS** in **10 MINUTES** while wearing **SKIS.**

ABOUT **10 PERCENT** OF THE WORLD'S FISH LIVE ON **AUSTRALIA'S GREAT BARRIER REEF.**

The **MOON** is **238,855 MILES** (384,400 km) away—about the same distance as traveling around the **EARTH 10 TIMES.**

There are **1.9 BILLION $10 BILLS** in circulation around the U.S.

10 -TASTIC FACTS!

At a **RACE** in the U.K., **RUNNERS** complete **10 MARATHONS IN 10 DAYS—** that's **262 MILES!** (422 km)

ABOUT EVERY **10 DAYS,** YOUR **TONGUE** REGENERATES ITS **TASTE BUDS.**

That's Weird!

One in **10 PET DOGS** have their own **SOCIAL MEDIA accounts,** according to a recent survey.

ITCHING IS CONTAGIOUS.

A **pop-up restaurant** in a California, U.S.A., dungeon offered customers a chance to **dine with rats.**

For $49.99, visitors to the Rat Café could eat while being surrounded by the rodents.

Theodore Roosevelt was saved from an assassin's bullet by a 50-page speech in his pocket.

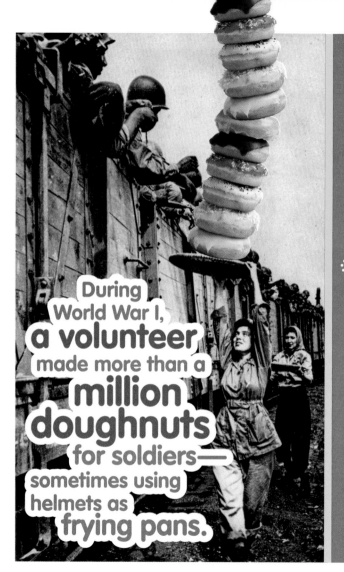

During World War I, **a volunteer** made more than a **million doughnuts** for soldiers— sometimes using helmets as **frying pans.**

A RUNAWAY PIG BLOCKED TRAFFIC FOR AN HOUR ON A BRIDGE IN MARYLAND, U.S.A.

A TERMITE QUEEN LAYS THOUSANDS OF EGGS EVERY DAY— MORE THAN A QUARTER BILLION IN HER LIFETIME.

A **VOLCANIC ERUPTION** IN INDONESIA ONCE MADE **SUMMER TEMPERATURES** IN CANADA DROP SO MUCH IT SNOWED.

At London's annual **Where's Waldo? race, runners** wear glasses and **red-and-white-striped shirts** to honor the famous **hidden book character.**

WHERE AM I?

Paleontologists found a fossilized rat skull the size of a hippopotamus.

A FORMER BRITISH SOCCER STAR SET A WORLD RECORD BY POSING FOR 134 SELFIES IN JUST THREE MINUTES!

ONE BRIDE AND GROOM RECENTLY HAD **SEVEN** WEDDINGS IN SEVEN COUNTRIES IN 40 DAYS.

TO TRICK POTENTIAL *THIEVES,* SQUIRRELS SOMETIMES PRETEND TO BURY A NUT.

A university in Georgia, U.S.A., has a collection of more than 1,000,000 ticks.

IN LESS THAN 15 MINUTES, CAMELS CAN DRINK ENOUGH WATER TO FILL A BATHTUB.

An **Italian company** grows **strawberries** and **tomatoes** in **undersea** greenhouses.

The first **dinosaurs** **with** **wings** **couldn't** **fly.**

WEALTHY RUSSIANS HIRED FAKE AMBULANCES TO GET THEM THROUGH MOSCOW'S TRAFFIC JAMS.

There's a **swimming pool** shaped like the **state of Texas** in Plano, Texas, U.S.A.

IN JAPAN, YOU CAN HIRE A PROFESSIONAL TO APOLOGIZE FOR YOU.

Bandits have stolen millions of dollars' worth of nuts in California.

ARTIFICIAL-INTELLIGENCE RESEARCHERS HAVE CREATED **SOUNDS** THAT **NO HUMAN** HAS EVER HEARD BEFORE.

The planet **KELT-11b** is larger than Jupiter but has the **density of a Styrofoam ball.**

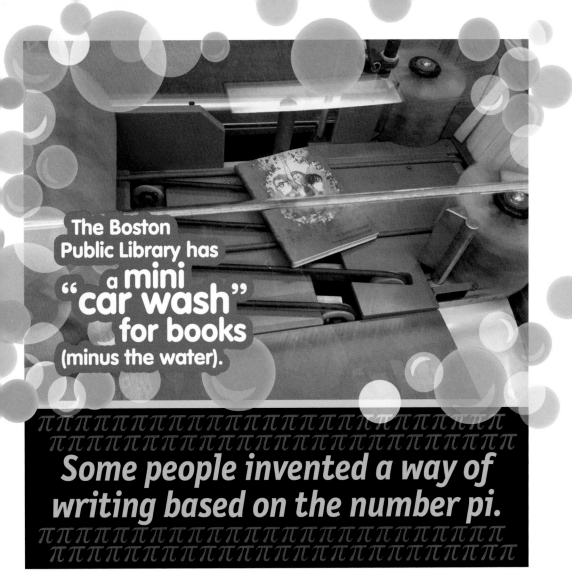

The Boston Public Library has a mini "car wash" for books (minus the water).

Some people invented a way of writing based on the number pi.

George Everest **never saw** the **mountain** that was named after him.

Penguins the size of a **12-year-old kid** waddled around Earth **61 million** years ago.

In Sweden, there is a **bakery** and a cheese-and-cracker shop made just for **mice.**

NOIX DE VIE

Turiststråket

SWEDEN HAS ITS OWN NATIONAL **FONT,** SWEDEN SANS.

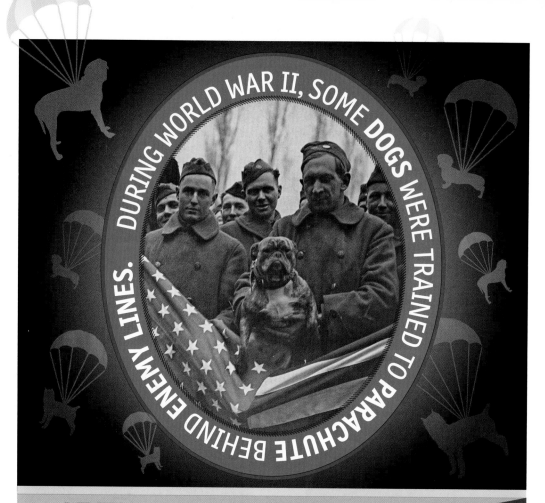

DURING WORLD WAR II, SOME **DOGS** WERE TRAINED TO **PARACHUTE** BEHIND ENEMY LINES.

YOUR **LIVER** **GROWS** DURING THE DAY, THEN **SHRINKS** AT NIGHT.

A medieval town sits at the bottom of a lake in Tuscany, Italy.

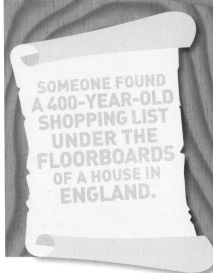

SOMEONE FOUND A 400-YEAR-OLD SHOPPING LIST UNDER THE FLOORBOARDS OF A HOUSE IN ENGLAND.

A Russian psychotherapist tried to hypnotize the entire Soviet Union by television.

Tortoise beetle larvae cover themselves in their own **poop** for protection.

Babies as young as **17 days old** can laugh.

A HUMPBACK WHALE'S SONG CAN LAST AS LONG AS 20 MINUTES AND IS OFTEN REPEATED FOR HOURS.

A Japanese artist made a **pair of shoes** that looked like **pigeons** so the birds wouldn't be **afraid of her.**

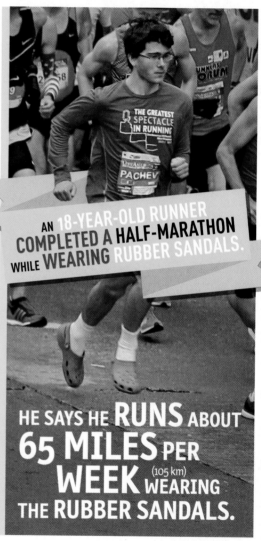

AN 18-YEAR-OLD RUNNER COMPLETED A HALF-MARATHON WHILE WEARING RUBBER SANDALS.

HE SAYS HE **RUNS** ABOUT **65 MILES** PER **WEEK** (105 km) WEARING THE **RUBBER SANDALS.**

A DAY ON THE PLANET VENUS IS LONGER THAN A YEAR ON VENUS.

Abstract **paintings** done by a four-year-old **dog** sell online for about **$40** each.

A **restaurant** in Michigan, U.S.A., serves a **hamburger** that weighs more than **300 pounds.**

(136 kg)

SPIDERS BUILT A 98-FOOT (30-m) WEB IN A NEW ZEALAND FIELD.

199

The "ice" in the first ice-skating rink was made of fat and salt.

GLACIARIUM.

(It smelled, and the rink closed in less than a year.)

Ears are self-cleaning.

Scientists turned a spinach leaf into human heart tissue.

A MAN IN AUSTRALIA BUILT A HOUSE OUT OF GARBAGE.

202

Fields of colorful **wildflowers** that **bloomed** in Southern California, U.S.A., could be seen **from space.**

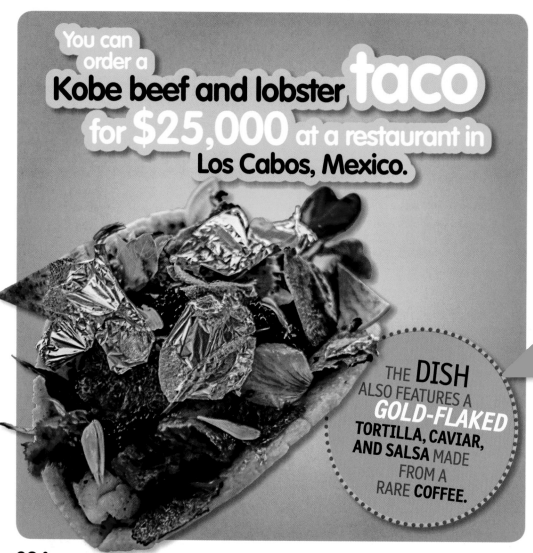

You can order a **Kobe beef and lobster taco** for **$25,000** at a restaurant in **Los Cabos, Mexico.**

THE **DISH** ALSO FEATURES A **GOLD-FLAKED TORTILLA, CAVIAR, AND SALSA** MADE FROM A RARE **COFFEE.**

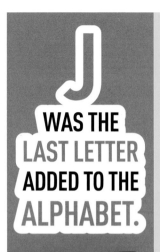

J WAS THE LAST LETTER ADDED TO THE ALPHABET.

In an **Alaska**, U.S.A., **neighborhood**, the street is a **runway**, and each house's " **garage** " is for an **airplane**.

Some bats can eat more than half their body weight in insects every day.

ABOUT
75 PERCENT OF ALL OCEAN

ANIMALS GLOW IN THE DARK.

FACTFINDER

Boldface indicates illustrations.

FACTFINDER

FACTFINDER

Front cover: anyamuse/Shutterstock; spine: ArchMan/Shutterstock; back cover: Filipe Frazao/Shutterstock; 2, anyamuse/Shutterstock; 4–5 (A), Duncan Noakes/Dreamstime; 4–5 (B), Richard Peterson/Shutterstock; 4–5 (C), Talvi/Shutterstock; 4–5 (D), gualtiero boffi/Shutterstock; 4–5 (E), tristan tan/Shutterstock; 4–5 (back), sirin.chan/Shutterstock; 6, Javed Ahmed, Rajashree Khalap, & Sumukha J.N./image by Sumukha J.N./lead researcher and principal author, Javed Ahmed; 8, Claudio Divizia/Shutterstock; 9 (UP RT), Courtesy Amber Marienthal; 9 (UP LE), duniascrap/Shutterstock; 10–11, John Kucko Digital; 13 (LO), gallofoto/Shutterstock; 13 (UP), Susan Schmitz/Shutterstock; 14–15 (LO), The Catboat Amsterdam; 15, Courtesy USGS; 16–17, Courtesy Dalene Zender/Heart of Texas Real Estate; 18, Bianca Lavies/National Geographic Creative; 21 (LE), Rachata Kietsirikul/Shutterstock; 21 (LO), viki2win/Shutterstock; 22–23, Jakub Cejpek/Shutterstock; 25, John Abbott/NPL/Minden Pictures; 26, Maurizio Savini, I Like America America Likes Me, 2007, chewed gum and fiberglass, 230 x 140 x 120 cm, Courtesy of Galleria Mucciaccia, Photography by Ottavio Celestine; 27, WesAbrams/Getty Images; 28 (LE), Eric Isselee/Shutterstock; 28 (RT), Eric Isselee/Shutterstock; 29, MonikaMPhotography/Getty Images; 30 (LO), Duncan Andison/Shutterstock; 30 (UP), Ayca Yalciner/Shutterstock; 31, Ozja/Shutterstock; 32, Cal Sport Media/Alamy Stock Photo; 34 (back), STANZI/Shutterstock; 35 (CTR), Hurst Photo/Shutterstock; 36, Jurgen Freund/NPL/Minden Pictures; 39, Eric Isselee/Shutterstock; 40, Lonely Planet Images/Getty Images; 42, Courtesy KFC New Zealand/YUM Brands; 43, Bacon Addicts; 44 (UP), mironov/Shutterstock; 44, Dmitry A/Shutterstock; 44 (LO), Kyodo/Newscom; 45 (RT), tanaphongpict/Shutterstock; 45 (LE), railway fx/Shutterstock; 46–47 (back), aaabbbccc/Shutterstock; 46 (LE), Marten_House/Shutterstock; 46 (RT), kovop58/Shutterstock; 47 (LE), feathercollector/Shutterstock; 47 (RT), Sergey Uryadnikov/Shutterstock; 48, Irina Rogova/Shutterstock; 50, Mike Parry/Minden Pictures; 51 (LE), Ron and Brenda Bailey; 51 (RT), Danny Smythe/Shutterstock; 52–53, blickwinkel/Alamy Stock Photo; 55, Dirk Ercken/Shutterstock; 56 (outer), Le Do/Shutterstock; 56 (inner), Ryzhkov Photography/Shutterstock; 56 (CTR), Bochkarev Photography/Shutterstock; 56–57, BW Folsom/Shutterstock; 58–59, coronado/Shutterstock; 60, solepsizm/Shutterstock; 61, Digital Construction Platform by Steven Keating, Julian Leland, Levi Cai, Prof. Neri Oxman; 63, NASA; 64–65, Fred Bavendam/Minden Pictures; 66 (UP), alfernec/Shutterstock; 66 (LO), Ttatty/Shutterstock; 67, Coaster/Alamy Stock Photo; 68, grafvision/Shutterstock; 69, dpa picture alliance archive/Alamy Stock Photo; 70, Orhan Cam/Shutterstock; 70 (LE), Library of Congress; 73, Norbert Wu/Minden Pictures; 76–77, Donna Heatfield/Shutterstock; 77 (LO), kritskaya/Shutterstock; 79, CPEN1/ZOB/Newscom; 80, Fernando Montealegre-Z; 81, David L. Ryan/The Boston Globe via Getty Images; 82–83 (LO), Brian Cahn/ZUMA Wire/Alamy Stock Photo; 82–83 (UP), Anan Kaewkhammul/Shutterstock; 84 (UP LE), Emily Seilhamer/Newscom; 84 (UP RT), Chones/Shutterstock; 84 (LO RT), Courtesy Weymouth Sea Life Park; 84 (LO LE), Sandy Buffie; 85 (UP), NASA; 85 (LO), Filipe Frazao/Shutterstock; 86, andersphoto/Shutterstock; 87, Bettmann Archive/Getty Images; 88–89, aaltair/Shutterstock; 90, Courtesy Everett Collection; 91, mdomingz18/Shutterstock; 92 (LE), Tin & Ed; 92 (UP RT), Matt Marut/Shutterstock; 92, Jagodka/Shutterstock; 94, Olga Popova/Shutterstock; 95, Bhakpong/Shutterstock; 96 (LE), Vivo Barefoot; 96 (RT), Jim Barber/Shutterstock; 97, Keystone-France/Getty Images; 100–101, Mark Moffett/Minden Pictures; 102, vovan/Shutterstock; 103, vovan/Shutterstock; 104, Guy Williams, University of Tasmania; 106–107, Sam Yeh/AFP/Getty Images; 109, Chris Hasson; 112–113, Peter Macdiarmid/Getty Images; 115, Biken; 116 (LE), Fidel/Shutterstock; 116, Antonio Gravante/Shutterstock; 117, Fred Harper; 118–119, iStockphoto/Getty Images; 120 (UP), Christopher MacDonald/Shutterstock; 120, Genuine Fred; 122, Anton Balazh/Shutterstock; 124, Eliot F. Gomez, Laboratory of Organic Electronics, Linköping University; 126 (UP LE), ilovehz/Shutterstock; 126 (UP RT), AFP/Getty Images/Getty Images; 126 (LO), AS photo studio/Shutterstock; 127 (RT), Portia Rollings; 127 (CTR), Joe Belanger/Shutterstock; 127 (LE), Joe Belanger/Shutterstock; 128, Bruno Pambour/Biosphoto/Minden Pictures; 130 (UP), Dave Walsh/VWPics/Newscom; 130 (LO), Bart van Hoek, Attika Architekten; 131, Universal Images Group Editorial/Getty Images; 132 (CTR), vovan/Shutterstock; 132 (LO), jorisvo/Shutterstock; 133, AP Photo; 134, Svetlana Isochenko/Alamy Stock Photo; 137, NASA; 139, Protasov AN/Shutterstock; 141, The Washington Post/Getty Images; 142–143, enny Dean/Rex Features/Shutterstock; 144, Antonio Bat/EPA/REX/Shutterstock; 147, NASA; 148–149, Frolova_Elena/Shutterstock; 151, Karen Bleier/AFP/Getty Images; 152, Fredrik von Erichsen/Newscom; 154–155, Owen Lin/Barcroft Images via Getty Images; 156, Thomas Rendleman/Pexels; 157 (LO), Shukaylova Zinaida/Shutterstock; 157 (UP), Picsfive/Shutterstock; 158, Jason Karl, Cornell University; 160–161, From sky to the Earth/Shutterstock; 163, Visual via ZUMA Press/Newscom; 164 (UP LE), Serjio74/Shutterstock; 164 (LO LE), Chris Cole / Allsport/Getty Images; 164 (UP RT), Cosmin Manci/Shutterstock; 164 (LO RT), Stocktrek Images/National Geographic Creative; 165 (LE), iStockphoto/Getty Images; 165 (RT), pramot/Shutterstock; 166–167, Lapina/Shutterstock; 169, Nataliia Zhekova/Shutterstock; 170 (main), Paul Popper/Popperfoto/Getty Images; 170 (UP), Mike Flippo/Shutterstock; 172–173, Tove Larsen/Alamy Stock Photo; 174, Andres Rinderknecht; 175, Mirrorpix/Newscom; 178, Nemo's Garden – Ocean Reef Group; 180, Franco Tempesta; 183, Courtesy Boston Public Library; 184–185, Daniel Prudek/Shutterstock; 186, Djomas/Shutterstock; 187 (UP), Pacific Press/Alamy Stock Photo; 187 (LO), Zoonar GmbH/Alamy Stock Photo; 188, Library of Congress; 189, Gino Santa Maria/Shutterstock; 190–191, Premaphotos/NPL/Minden Pictures; 192, Peter Young/Getty Images; 194, Matt Kryger/IndyStar; 196–197, Courtesy Shiba Art Online; 198, WENN.com/Newscom; 200, Corbin Historical/Getty Images; 201 (UP), Vladimir Gjorgiev/Shutterstock; 201 (LO), Jiri Hera/Shutterstock; 202–203, NASA; 204, Courtesy Grand Velas Los Cabos, KWE Partners; 206 (LO), David Shale/NPL/Minden Pictures; 206 (UP RT), David Shale/NPL/Minden Pictures; 206 (UP LE), Doug Perrine/NPL/Minden Pictures; 207 (LO LE), Gabriel Barathieu/Biosphoto/Minden Pictures; 207 (UP LE), Constantinos Petrinos/NPL/Minden Pictures; 207 (LO RT), Norbert Wu/Minden Pictures; 207 (UP RT), Karl Van Ginderdeuren/Buiten-beeld/Minden Pictures

ISBN 978-1-338-33878-2

12 11 10 9 8 7 6 5 4 3 2 1   18 19 20 21 22 23

Printed in the U.S.A.   40

First Scholastic printing, November 2018

Designed by Rachael Hamm Plett, Moduza Design

The publisher would like to thank Avery Hurt, researcher; Sarah Wassner Flynn, researcher; Grace Hill Smith, project editor; Paige Towler, project manager; Kathryn Robbins, art director; Hillary Leo, photo editor; and Lori Epstein, photo director.

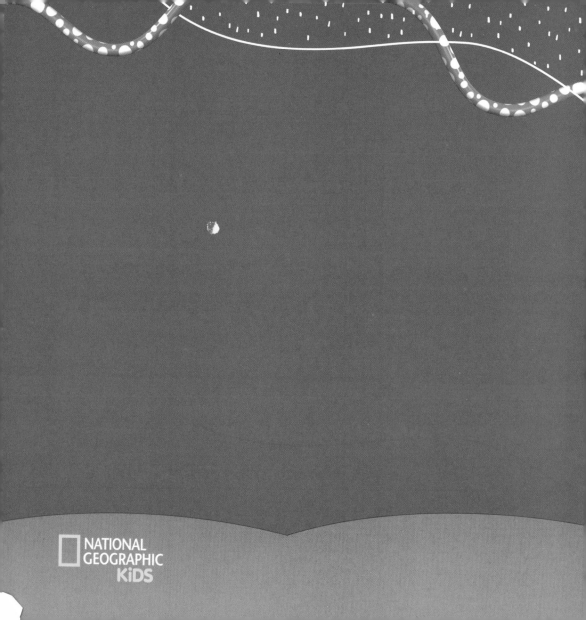